Collins Primary S

NURSERY RHYMES

Linda Howe

Resources Needed

Collections To Be Made

Toys (2)

Fruits with and without pips (3)

Different sizes of bags (5)

Different sizes of containers (6)

Magnetic and non-magnetic objects (7)

General Resources

Paper (1,2,3,4,11)

Rubber bands (1)

Wax crayons (1)

Sand (1)

Plasticine (1)

Bag/pillow case (2)

Pencils (2,3,4)

Knife (3)

Crayons (4)

Magazines and catalogues (4)

Balances (5)

Different materials (5)

Chalk (6)

Magnets (7)

Card (7,14)

Paper clips (7)

Glue (11,12)

Scissors (11)

Greaseproof paper (14)

Mirrors (14)

Sticks (7)

Yoghurt pots (8,12)

Soil (8)

Sand (8)

Salt (8,9)

Bun tins (10)

Cotton material (11)

Plastic bottles (12,14)

Margarine tubs (12)

String (12,14)

Fillings (12)

Lengths of wood (13)

Building blocks (13)

Weights (13)

Funnels (14)

Other Resources

Plaster of Paris (1)

Cress seeds (8)

Self-raising flour (9)

Baking powder (9)

Pastry mix (10)

Jam (10)

Pastry cutters (8,10)

Dried lavender/pot pourri (11)

Pieces of ribbon (11)

Face paints (14)

Cold cream (14)

Contents

	Resources needed	2
1	Cock-a-Doodle-Doo	4
2	Boys and Girls	6
3	Counting rhymes	8
4	Twinkle, Twinkle	10
5	Baa, Baa Black Sheep	12
6	Incy, Wincy Spider	14
7	One, Two, Three, Four, Five	16
8	Mary, Mary Quite Contrary	18
9	Pat-a-Cake	20
10	The Queen of Hearts	22
11	Lavender's Blue	24
12	Little Boy Blue	26
13	See-Saw Margery Daw	28
14	Teddy Bears' Picnic	30
	Acknowledgements	32

1 COCK-A-DOODLE-DO

Cock-a-Doodle-Doo,
   My dame has lost her shoe;
My master's lost his fiddling stick
   And doesn't know what to do.

If you lost one of your new shoes how would you describe it to someone helping to look for it?

Take off one shoe and look at it closely.
What colour is it? Is it the same all over? Does it have any patterns, holes or scuff marks?
How does it fasten? Does it have laces, buckles or Velcro?
What else do you notice?

SOMETHING TO TRY

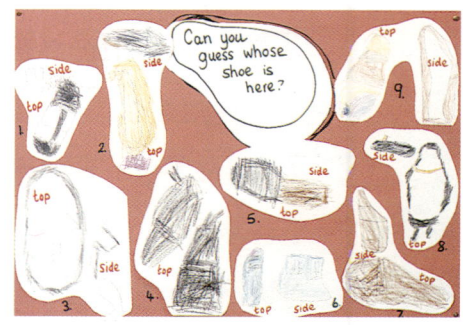

Everyone should draw the top and side views of their shoes without writing their name on their pictures. Mix up the drawings. Can you match the drawings to the shoes? Are there any which look just the same?

Look at the undersides of the shoes. Do they have patterns or writing on them? Rub your hand over the shoe bottoms. Do they feel rough or smooth, bumpy or flat?

Making patterns with shoes

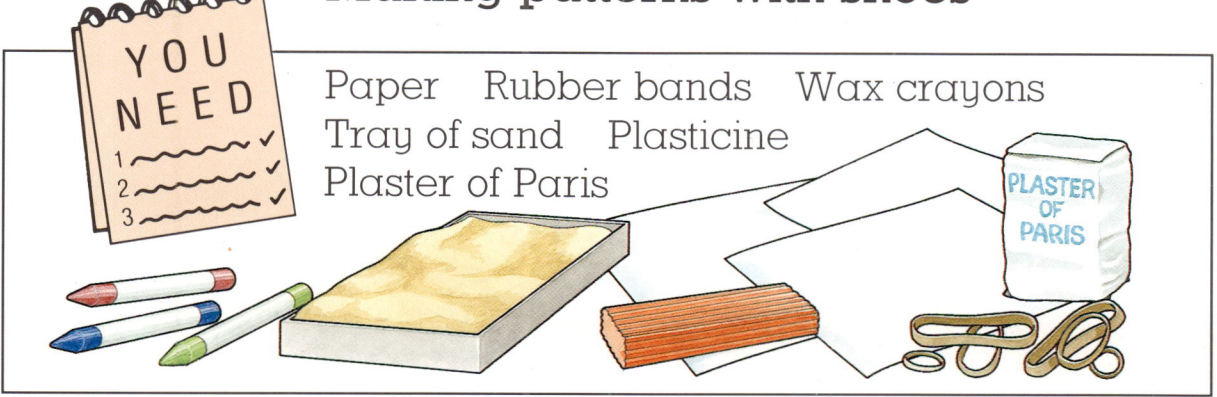

YOU NEED: Paper, Rubber bands, Wax crayons, Tray of sand, Plasticine, Plaster of Paris

Press your shoe in a tray of sand. Does it leave a mark? Try both wet and dry sand.

Put a piece of paper over the underside of your shoe, using a rubber band to help hold it still. Rub lightly over the paper with the side of a wax crayon. You can then take the paper off, smooth it out and cut out the shoe shape.

Make a flat pancake shape with Plasticine. Press your shoe on the Plasticine. Does it leave a pattern? Build a Plasticine wall around the pattern. Put some water in a bowl and sprinkle plaster of Paris onto the water until no more will soak in. Stir and pour the mixture on to the Plasticine. Leave it to set for about one hour and then carefully remove the mould.

Next day the plaster of Paris will be hard enough to colour over with wax crayons or thick paint. It will look good if just the bumps are coloured.

BOYS AND GIRLS

Boys and girls come out to play,
   The moon does shine as bright as day;
Leave your supper and leave your sleep,
   Join your playmates in the street.

Can you find any pictures of old-fashioned toys?
You might be able to visit a local museum or borrow some old toys to look at.
How do you think toys have changed?
Can you find out about toys and games that your grannies or grandads had?

Draw a picture of your favourite toy.
What is it made from?
What colour is it?
Do any parts move?
What else can you say about it?

The first people probably lived in caves.
They would have had to use things around them for toys.
Small stones and fruits could be used as balls, sticks on logs for drums and bits of wood as rafts.
Can you think of some other things that could have been used?

Some guessing games with toys

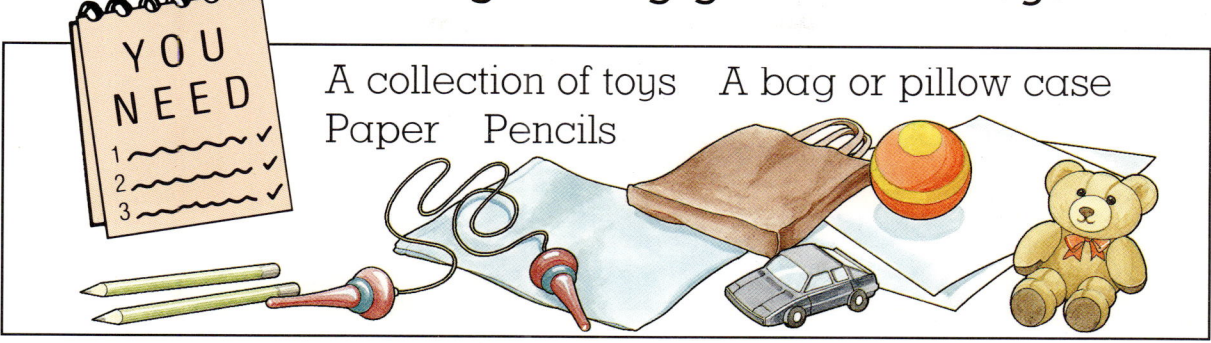

YOU NEED: A collection of toys   A bag or pillow case   Paper   Pencils

Sit in a circle and put one of the toys in a bag or pillow case without anyone seeing it. Six children from the circle can put their hands in the bag to feel the toy. Can they say if it is big or small, hard or soft, heavy or light, warm or cold, flat or bumpy, squashy or firm? Can you think of any other questions to ask? Can you guess which toy is in the bag?

Ask one child to think of either their favourite toy or one of the toys in the class collection. They must not tell anyone which toy they have chosen. Everyone else should have paper and pencils. The child then has to describe the toy they have chosen for everyone to draw. Which drawing do they think is closest? They can then tell everyone what it is and let someone else have a turn. Do the drawings get better?

The drawings can be displayed around a picture of the actual toy.

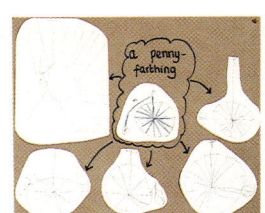

COUNTING RHYMES

Tinker, Tailor
   Soldier, Sailor
Rich man, Poor man
   Beggar man, Thief!

One for sorrow, two for joy,
   Three for a girl, four for a boy,
Five for silver, six for gold,
   Seven for a secret never to be told.

Do you ever eat fruit with stones in and say a counting poem with the stones? You might know more than the two above.

Can you find out which fruits have stones or pips inside?

YOU NEED: A collection of different fruits   Paper   Pencils   A knife

ACTIVITY -A- Sit in a circle. Put the fruit in the middle. Choose one piece of fruit and pass it around. Is it round or long, big or little, rough or smooth, bumpy or flat, hard or squashy? What colours can you see? What else can you say about it?

ACTIVITY -B- Choose one piece of fruit and take a piece of paper and a pencil.

Fold the piece of paper into three and then open it out. In one part draw the outside of the fruit. In the middle part draw what you think the fruit will look like when it is cut open.

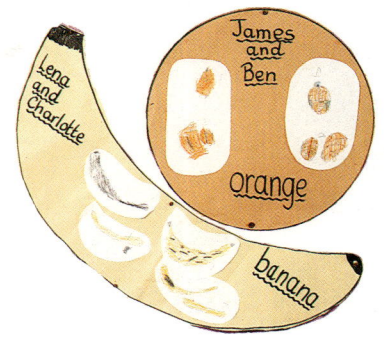

Do you think it will have a stone or pips? Cut open the fruit and draw what it looks like cut open on the last part of the paper. Is this drawing the same as your middle drawing?

Use the fruits to make some sets. You could try:
- shapes
- sizes
- colours
- with stalks and without stalks
- with pips or stones and without pips or stones

You could also try your own ideas.

Try planting the pips and stones that you have found. Which ones do you think will grow?

Make some labels to show which fruits the seeds came from. You could stick your labels onto sticks (cocktail sticks) and put them in the pots next to the seeds.

The drawings form the record and could be used to make sets.

TWINKLE, TWINKLE

Twinkle, twinkle little star,
   How I wonder what you are;
Up above the world so high,
   Like a diamond in the sky.

Think of something that you enjoy doing on a nice, sunny day.
Could you do the same thing in the middle of the night?
Why not?

Some people might be working while you are asleep, like the police, ambulance drivers, doctors and nurses and the fire service. Can you think of some others?

Some people start work very early like farm workers, milk deliverers and postmen and women. Can you think of others?

Make up a story about what it is like to work when most people are in bed.

Thinking about day and night

YOU NEED   Magazines and catalogues   Paper   Pencils   Crayons

ACTIVITY -A-

Draw two large circles on a piece of paper.
Write *day* above one circle and *night* above the other.
Draw things that you do in the day and things that you do at night in the right circles.
Can you think of more daytime or more nightime things? Why do you think this is?

ACTIVITY -B-

When it is dark we use lights to help us see. Think of as many different places where we use lights as you can.
Look in the magazines and catalogues for pictures of lights. Make sets of indoor and outdoor lights.

SOMETHING TO FIND OUT

Some animals sleep during the day and come out at night. Can you find out the names of any?

RECORDING

The drawings form the main record. You could make a class book of animals and birds that sleep during the day.

BAA, BAA BLACK SHEEP

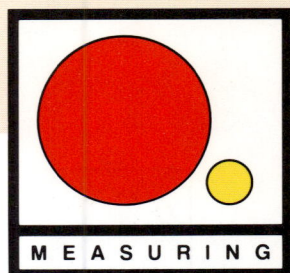

MEASURING

Baa, baa, black sheep
   Have you any wool?
Yes sir, yes sir,
   Three bags full.

Do you bring a bag to school?
What do you carry in it?
Draw or write a list of all the things in your bag. Do you bring the same things every day?

Can you think of some more bags, such as:
a handbag, a shopping bag, a sports bag, a laundry bag, a swimming bag?

For each one you think of, can you say where it is used and what is put in it?
Why do we use bags?
What would it be like to try and carry your shopping home without a bag?

What is a bag full?

YOU NEED

Different sizes of bags   Balances
A selection of materials

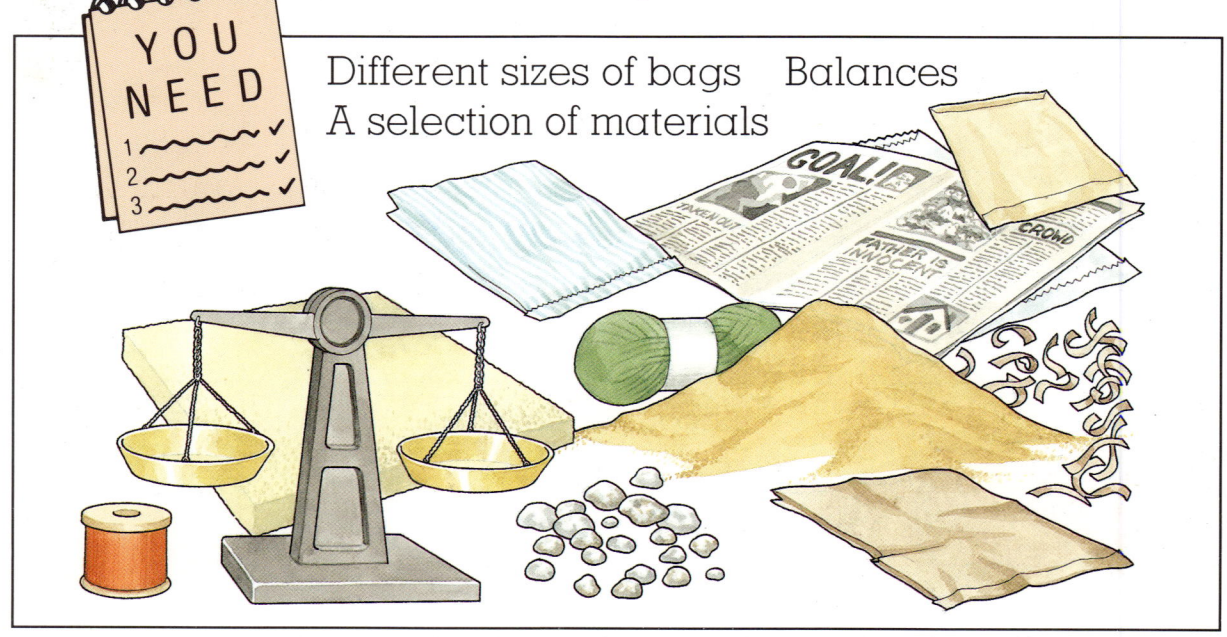

Sort the bags in order of size
(big to little).
Choose the biggest bag.
How many sheets of newspaper do you think it will hold? Can you find out if you guessed the right number?
Try some other bags. For each one guess how many sheets it will hold before trying it.

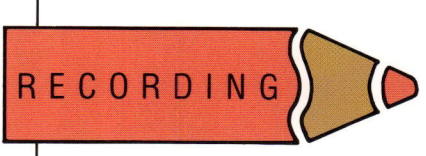 Make a chart to show how many sheets of newspaper each bag held.

Choose one bag. How much newspaper did it hold? Fill the bag with sand and then tip the sand from the bag into  one side of the balances. Now fill the bag with something squashy like wool or foam. Does it hold more or less of this than sand? Put it on the other side of the balances and see which side is heaviest. Try some other things in the same way.

 Make a chart to show the bags in order of weight.

INCY, WINCY SPIDER

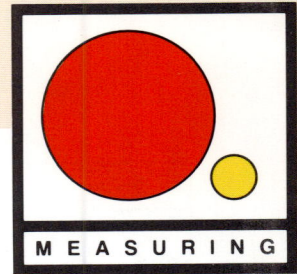
MEASURING

Incy, Wincy Spider climbing up the spout,
   Down came the rain and washed the spider out;
Out came the sun and dried up all the rain,
   Incy, Wincy Spider climbs up the spout again.

Do you like rainy days?
What do you like doing on wet days?
Do you wear special clothing?
Do you wear a raincoat, a rainhat or wellingtons?
Do you have an umbrella?
Draw a picture of yourself in the rain.

There are many stories about rainy days.
Make up your own story about a rainy day.
What would happen if it went on raining and raining without stopping?
What would it be like if we never had any rain?
What would it be like if it rained lemonade instead of water?

How long do puddles take to dry?

YOU NEED
Different sizes of containers
Water   Chalk   A dry playground

 **ACTIVITY** Use the different containers full of water to make some puddles on the playground. You should make your puddles in different places on the playground.

You might be able to find some sunny places and some shady places. Use the chalk to draw around the edges of the puddles. Are all the puddles the same size? (Number them by size.) Can you find out how long the puddles take to dry? Do big puddles dry more quickly than small ones? Do puddles in the sun dry more quickly than puddles in the shade? Which part of a puddle dries first – the edges or the middle?

RECORDING Make a chart to show the drying times of the puddles.

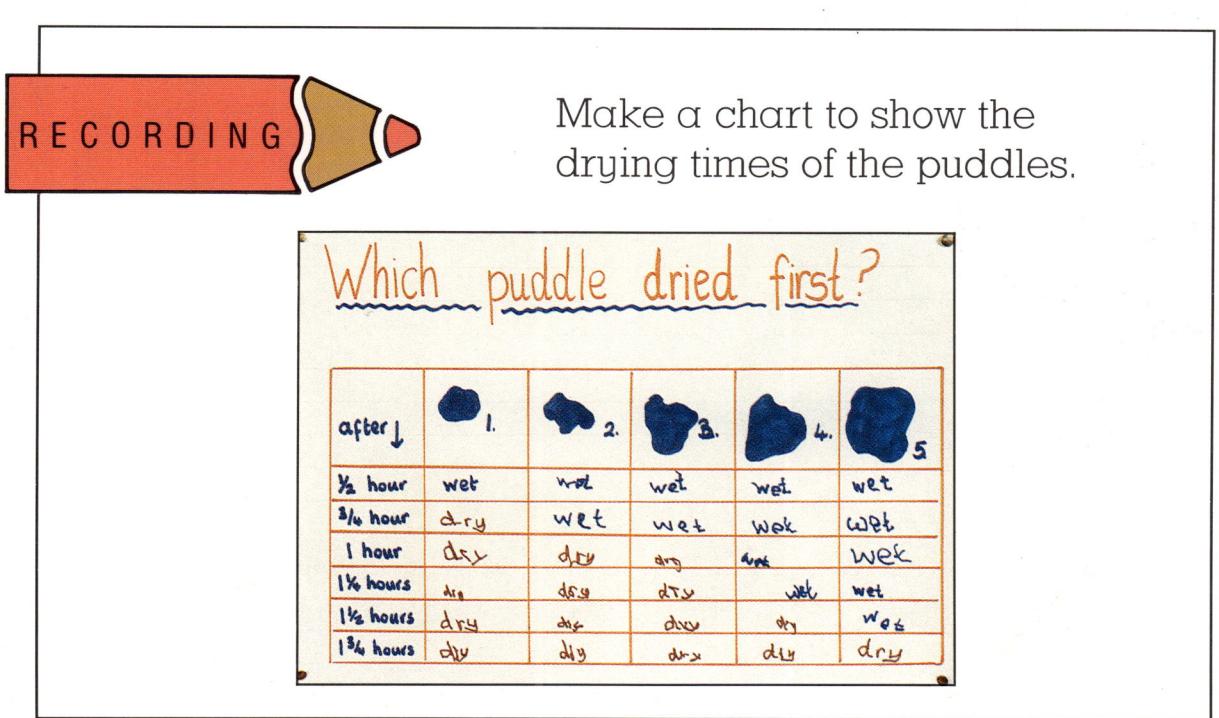

Which puddle dried first?

after ↓	1.	2.	3.	4.	5.
½ hour	wet	wet	wet	wet	wet
¾ hour	dry	wet	wet	wet	wet
1 hour	dry	dry	dry	wet	wet
1¼ hours	dry	dry	dry	wet	wet
1½ hours	dry	dry	dry	dry	wet
1¾ hours	dry	dry	dry	dry	dry

ONE, TWO, THREE, FOUR, FIVE

'One, two, three, four, five,
  Once I caught a fish alive,
Six, seven, eight, nine, ten,
  Then I let it go again.'
'Why did you let it go?'
  'Because it bit my finger so.'
'Which finger did it bite?'
  'This little finger on my right.'

Making a magnetic fish game

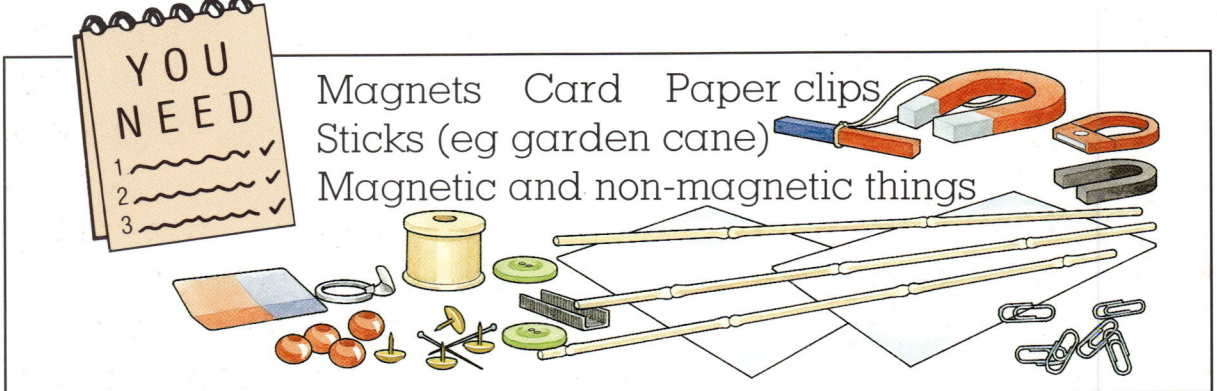

YOU NEED: Magnets   Card   Paper clips
Sticks (eg garden cane)
Magnetic and non-magnetic things

ACTIVITY -A-

Find out which things the magnets will pick up. Using a magnet, make a set of things which it will pick up and a set of things which it will not pick up.

What kinds of things are in the sets? Can you find any things which the magnet will pick up which are not metal? Can you find any metal things which the magnet will not pick up?

ACTIVITY -B-

Test to find out which magnet is the strongest. Choose one of the magnets. How many paper clips will it pick up at once? Now try with the other magnets. Which magnet will pick up the most paper clips? You could try wrapping the magnets in paper. How many sheets will the magnets work through?

ACTIVITY -C-

Cut out some card fish shapes and put a paper clip on each one. Put the fish in the middle of a table or on the floor. Make a magnetic fishing rod by tying a magnet to one end of a piece of string and the other end to a stick. How many fish can you catch with your magnetic rod? How quickly can you catch all the fish?

RECORDING

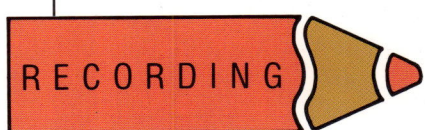

Draw sets of magnetic and non-magnetic objects. Make a chart to show the strongest magnet.

MARY, MARY QUITE CONTRARY

'Mary, Mary Quite Contrary
   How does your garden grow?'
'With silver bells,
   And cockle shells,
And pretty maids all in a row.'

Go for a walk around your school grounds or in the park. How many different plants can you find growing? How do you know that they are different? Look out for different leaf shapes, colours, flowers, leaf sizes.
What else could you look out for?

How many different places can you find with plants growing in them? You might see:

trees or a hedge   flowers in a bed   grass on a field

weeds   moss on a wall

Sometimes plants even grow on a roof. How many can you find?

Testing to find out where plants grow best

YOU NEED
Seeds (cress are quickest growing)   Soil
Small pots such as yoghurt pots   Sand   Salt

ACTIVITY -A-

Make a test to show where plants grow best. Try planting some seeds in pots, choosing different places to put them. You could try outside in a sunny place, outside in the shade, on the windowsill, in a cupboard, in a fridge, in a boiler room. Where else could you try? Water the seeds every day. Watch carefully to find out which seeds grow first and which you think grow best. Talk about why this might be.

ACTIVITY -B-

Test to find out how plants like to be treated. Try planting some seeds in:
- wet soil
- dry soil
- no soil
- wet sand
- dry sand
- under lots of soil
- in soil mixed with salt

What else could you try?

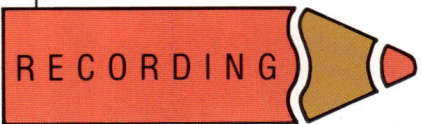

RECORDING

You could make a chart to show how well each plant grew.

PAT-A-CAKE

Pat-a-cake, pat-a-cake,
  Baker's man,
Bake me a cake as fast as you can.
  Pat it and prick it and mark it with B
And put it in the oven for baby and me.

Think of all the things that you might find in a baker's shop. It might sell bread, pies, sausage rolls, cakes, biscuits and scones. Can you think of some other things it might sell?

Make a class baker's shop with play dough bread

YOU NEED
1.5kg self-raising flour   1 kg salt
100g baking powder

Mix the ingredients with water to make a stiff dough. Use the play dough to make different shaped loaves and buns. Try:

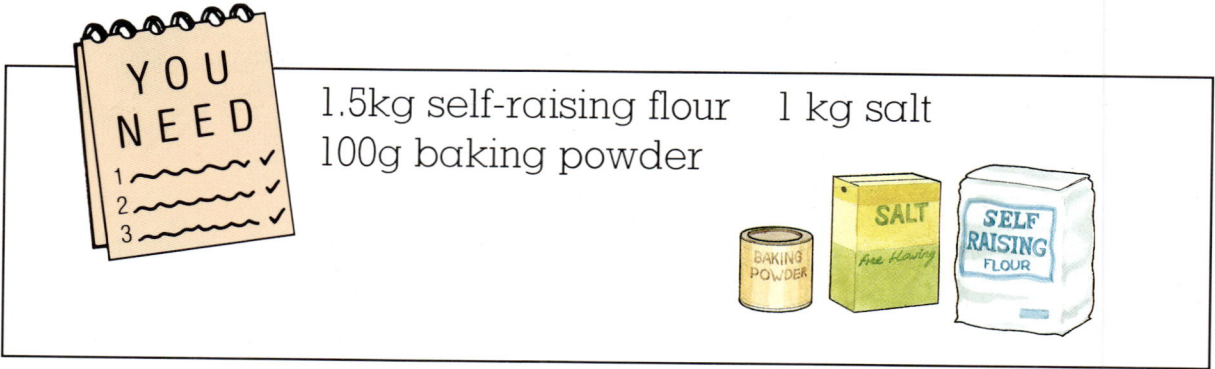

round   long   flat

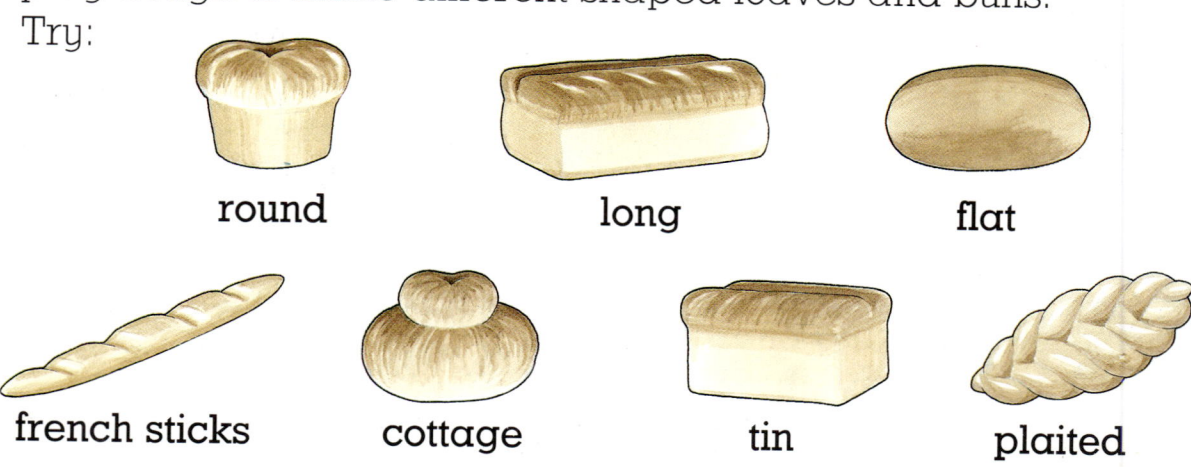

french sticks   cottage   tin   plaited

Brush the loaves with milk and bake in a hot oven (200°c). Do not eat the bread.

Which mixes keep their shape when cooked?

YOU NEED: Scone, cake, biscuit and pastry mixes
Baking trays

ACTIVITY

Write the first letter of your name on a piece of scrap paper. Use the mixture to make your letter shape on a baking tray. If you have a scone, biscuit or pastry mix you can use your fingers. If you have cake mix you will need a spoon. Cook the shapes in an oven. Do you think that you will still be able to see your letter shape when it is cooked?

When they are ready take the trays out of the oven and see which letter shapes you can find. Has anything else happened to the letter shapes?

RECORDING

A piece of paper folded in half can show the letter shape one side and the results the other.

THE QUEEN OF HEARTS

The Queen of Hearts
    She made some tarts
All on a summer's day;
    The Knave of Hearts
He stole those tarts
    And took them clean away.

Can you find some more verses of this rhyme which tell the rest of the story? Perhaps you might like to make up your own ending. How do you think the Queen felt when she found the tarts had gone? Do you think that the Knave was sorry?

Do you like jam tarts?
What is your favourite colour jam tart?
What flavour might it be if the jam is:
- red?
- green?
- yellow?
- orange?

Can you think of any other colours that jam tarts might be?
What else do you eat which is made of pastry or has jam in it?

Making jam tarts

YOU NEED

Pastry mix   Pastry cutters   Tart tins
Flour   A spoon   Rolling pins   Jam
A small skewer or fork

ACTIVITY

Try making some tarts in different ways:
You could:

1 Roll out the pastry and cut out some circles. Put the circles in the tins and put a spoonful of jam in the middle of each pastry circle and cook.

2 Roll out the pastry and cut out some circles as before. Put half the circles in the tin and cook them. Prick the remaining pastry circles with a skewer or fork and put them in a tin and cook them. Fill these tarts with jam after they are cooked. What do you notice about the pricked and unpricked pastry? Why do you think they are different?

Which way of cooking jam tarts do you like best?

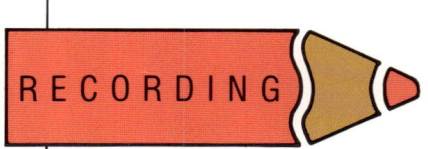

RECORDING

A class survey of favourite cooking methods could be made into a graph.

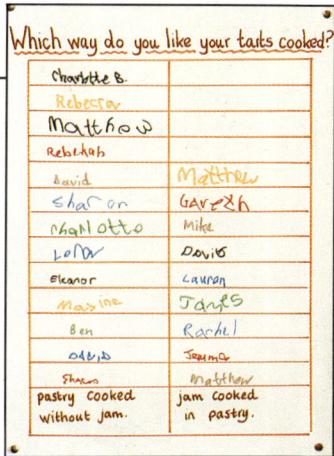

11 LAVENDER'S BLUE

Lavender's blue, Dilly, Dilly,
   Lavender's green;
When you are King, Dilly, Dilly,
   I shall be Queen.

Can you find a lavender plant to smell? If not, perhaps you could find some dried lavender or some soap, perfume or talcum powder which smells of lavender.

Lavender is used in bath water to make people's skin feel fresh and smell nice. It is hung in wardrobes and put in cupboards and chests full of clothes and sheets. Why do you think that people do this?

Bunches of lavender were sometimes hung in the house to keep insects out. Some insects do not like the smell of lavender. Women sold bunches of lavender in towns. They would call out, "Who will buy my sweet lavender?" Can you think of some other things which might be sold in the streets? Make up your own cries to tell everyone what you are selling.

Making a lavender bag

YOU NEED

Dried lavender or pot pourri   Paper
Cotton material   Glue   Scissors
Small pieces of ribbon

 Make a lavender bag to hang in your wardrobe. You should draw a shape that would look nice on a piece of paper. You could try:

heart   oblong   diamond

sock   butterfly   flower

Cut out your shape and use it as a pattern to cut out two material shapes.
Glue around the edge of one of your material shapes, leaving a small gap.

Stick the two pieces of material together and stuff the bag with lavender.
Once the bag is full glue up the gap and add a piece of ribbon to hang the bag by.

 The street cries can be written down or tape recorded. The pattern can be put in your project folder.

LITTLE BOY BLUE

Little Boy Blue, come blow up your horn;
  Sheep's in the meadow, cow's in the corn;
But where is the boy who looks after the sheep?
  He's under the haystack fast asleep.

Long ago children were given jobs to do on farms like looking after the sheep, picking up potatoes and scaring birds. To scare birds off the new seeds they would have a big rattle which made a loud noise. How else do you think people can stop birds eating their seeds?

Sometimes they make scarecrows. You could make a scarecrow or a scarecrow picture. Sometimes people hang up old cans and pieces of shiny paper. Sometimes they use a net. Automatic bird scarers make a loud bang every now and then. Why might these things scare the birds?

Making a loud rattle

YOU NEED

Plastic bottles   Yoghurt pots   Margarine tubs etc.   String   A variety of fillings   Strong glue   Dowel

 **ACTIVITY**

Think about making a rattle. Can you think of something to use that will make a loud noise? Can you think of a way to make the rattle easy to shake? You could try:

Draw a picture of what you hope your rattle will look like. Collect everything you will need and make your rattle. Did you need to change anything? Draw a picture of your finished rattle.

 **RECORDING**

The drawings of your plan and the completed rattle can form a record. Photographs would be useful.

SEE-SAW MARGERY DAW

INVESTIGATING

See-Saw Margery Daw,
   Johnny shall have a new master,
He shall have but a penny a day,
   Because he can't work any faster.

Is there a playground near your school? Does it have see-saws, slides, swings, climbing frames and roundabouts? Can you think of other things it has?

Do you have PE apparatus at school? How many different ways can you move on it? Can you:

crawl?   balance?   slide?   hang?

walk?   swing?   jump?   climb?

What else can you do?

Can you think of some other ways to move? You can run, hop, skip, swim and ride a bike.
How else can you move?

Finding out about see-saws

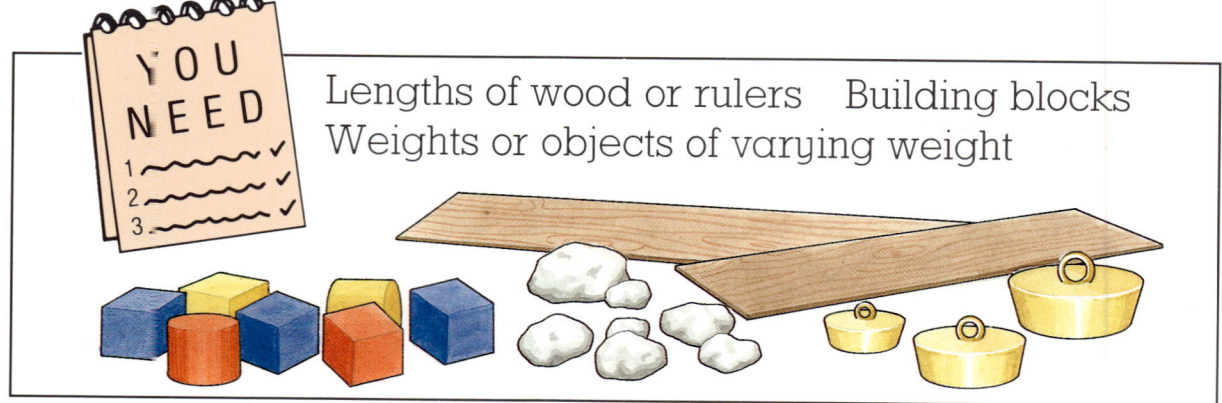

YOU NEED   Lengths of wood or rulers   Building blocks
Weights or objects of varying weight

28

 Take a ruler and a building block. Can you make a see-saw? Take two identical weights and put one on each end of the see-saw. Does it balance? Try moving the block nearer to one end and putting the weights on the ends. Does it balance now? Keep changing the position of the block. Does it have to be in the middle to balance?

 Try changing the weights. What happens if you use a big and a little weight? Does the block have to be in the middle to balance? Try different places for the block with different weights.

 Try different shapes of block as well as ideas of your own.

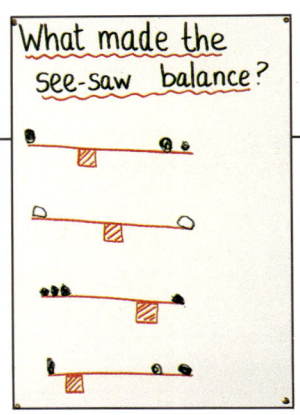

 You can draw some pictures to show what happened to the see-saws.

TEDDY BEARS' PICNIC

INVESTIGATING

If you go down to the woods today
    You'll be sure of a big surprise;
If you go down in the woods today
    You'd better go in disguise;
For every bear that ever there was
    Is gathered there for certain because
Today's the day the teddy bears have their picnic.

Disguising yourself

YOU NEED: Mirrors   Face paints or make-up   Cold cream   Combs   Paper   Plastic sunglasses   Card   Wool   String   Greaseproof paper   Funnels   Plastic bottles

ACTIVITY -A- Look in the mirror. Fold a piece of paper in half and open it out. On one half draw a picture of your face, using the mirror to help. Now can you change your face? Can you make it look cross, happy, worried, funny or sad? On the other half of the paper draw a picture of how your face looks now. How has your face changed?

RECORDING   The pictures form a record.

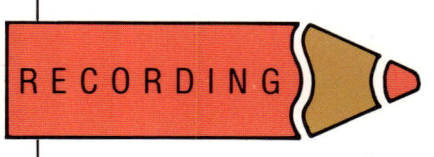

Can you change your face by using the face paints or make-up? What would you need to do to make a clown's face or a monster's face? Perhaps you could comb your hair in a different way or make a wig with string or wool. You could make a false beard or moustache and wear a pair of sunglasses. Would anyone recognise you now? Can you think of anything else to change the way you look?

You could take photographs of each other.

Can you change your voice? Try:
- talking in a high or gruff voice
- talking through a funnel or a plastic bottle with the end cut out.
- talking through a comb wrapped in greaseproof paper

What else could you try?

Use a tape recorder to record your different voices.

Acknowledgements

Copyright © 1990 Linda Howe
Reprinted 1991
ISBN 0 00 317541 3

Published by Collins Educational London and Glasgow
A division of HarperCollins

Design by David Bennett Books Ltd.
Illustrations by Amelia Rosato and Sally Neave
Commissioned photography by Oliver Hatch
Picture Research by Nance Fyson and Gwenan Morgan

Typeset by Kalligraphic Design Ltd., Horley, Surrey
Printed and bound in Hong Kong

All rights reserved. No part of this book may be reproduced or transmitted in any form or by any means, without the prior permission of the publisher.

The publishers thank St. John's First and Middle School, Ealing, London and Woolpit County Primary School, Suffolk for their kind co-operation in the production of Collins Primary Science.